The Rise of Nationalism:
The Arab World,
Turkey, and Iran

The Making of the Middle East

The Rise of Nationalism: The Arab World, Turkey, and Iran

Jonathan Spyer and Cameron Brown

Mason Crest Publishers
Philadelphia

Frontispiece: Arabs walk through the streets of East Jerusalem. Nationalism is the desire by people who share cultural or ethnic characteristics to rule their own independent state.

Produced by OTTN Publishing, Stockton, N.J.

Mason Crest Publishers
370 Reed Road
Broomall, PA 19008
www.masoncrest.com

First printing

1 3 5 7 9 8 6 4 2

Library of Congress Cataloging-in-Publication Data

Spyer, Jonathan.
   The rise of nationalism : the Arab World, Turkey, and Iran / Jonathan Spyer and Cameron Brown.
       p. cm. — (The making of the Middle East)
   Includes bibliographical references and index.
   ISBN-13: 978-1-4222-0169-5
   ISBN-10: 1-4222-0169-4
   1. Nationalism—Middle East. 2. Arab nationalism. 3. Nationalism—Turkey. 4. Nationalism—Iran. I. Brown, Cameron, 1976- II. Title.
   DS63.5.S69 2007
   320.540956—dc22
                                        2007024576

Table of Contents

Introduction:
The Importance of the Middle East

The region known as the Middle East has a significant impact on world affairs. The countries of the greater Middle East—the Arab states of the Arabian Peninsula, Eastern Mediterranean, and North Africa, along with Israel, Turkey, Iran, and Afghanistan—possess a large portion of the world's oil, a valuable commodity that is the key to modern economies. The region also gave birth to three of the world's major faiths: Judaism, Christianity, and Islam.

In recent years it has become obvious that events in the Middle East affect the security and prosperity of the rest of the world. But although such issues as the wars in Iraq and Afghanistan, the floundering Israeli-Palestinian peace process, and the struggles within countries like Lebanon and Sudan are often in the news, few Americans understand the turbulent history of this region.

Human civilization in the Middle East dates back more than 8,000 years, but in many cases the modern conflicts and issues in the region can be attributed to events and decisions made during the past 150 years. In particular, after World War I ended in 1918, the victorious Allies—especially France and Great Britain—redrew the map of the Middle East, creating a number of new countries, such as Iraq, Jordan, and Syria. Other states, such as Egypt and Iran, were dominated by foreign powers until after the Second World War. Many of the Middle Eastern countries did not become independent until the 1960s or 1970s. Political and economic developments in the Middle Eastern states over the past four decades have shaped the region's direction and led to today's headlines.

The purpose of the MAKING OF THE MIDDLE EAST series is to nurture a better understanding of this critical region, by providing the basic history along

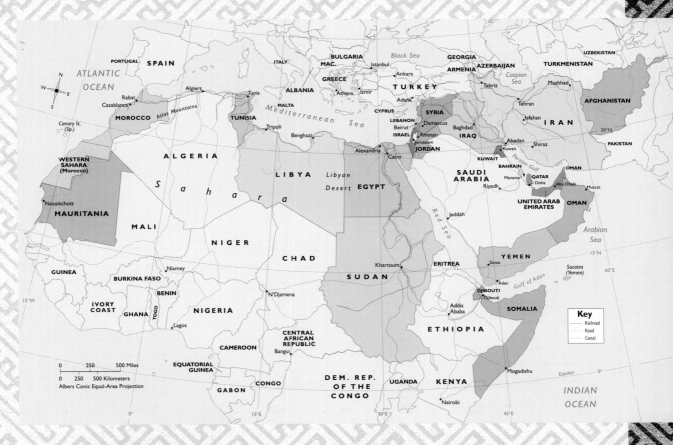

with explanation and analysis of trends, decisions, and events. Books will examine important movements in the Middle East, such as the development of nationalism in the 1880s and the rise of Islamism from the 1970s to the present day.

The 10 volumes in the MAKING OF THE MIDDLE EAST series are written in clear, accessible prose and are illustrated with numerous historical photos and maps. The series should spark students' interest, providing future decision-makers with a solid foundation for understanding an area of critical importance to the United States and the world.

Nationalities are often united by their religious beliefs. (Opposite) A mosque in Cairo, Egypt. Most Arabs follow Islam, a religion founded on the Arabian Peninsula nearly 1400 years ago. (Right) A scroll containing the Torah, or Hebrew scriptures. Despite thousands of years of persecution, the Jews have survived while other ancient nations have disappeared from history.

1 *Nationalism in the Middle East*

*T*he Middle East consists of 23 countries from three different continents. Most of these nations, such as Jordan, Syria, Lebanon, Iraq, Israel, and Iran, lie within the continent of Asia. But the Middle East also includes Turkey, whose northwestern part is in Europe, as well as countries from Africa, such as Egypt, Libya, and Algeria.

The Middle East is one of the most fractious and politically unstable regions of the world. In this region issues of identity, loyalty, tradition, and differing perceptions of history greatly affect peoples' lives. One of the most incendiary and central elements of the political culture of the modern Middle East has been the presence of nationalist ideology.

What Is Nationalism?

Nationalism is often defined as the advocacy for political independence. But it can also be described as a collective identity based on a combination of factors including family lineage (identification with families, clans, or tribes), geographical location, religion, and language. Throughout history, nationalism has been the inspiration for independence movements, driving the desire of various peoples to achieve self-rule, or autonomy.

In the Middle East, Arab civilizations dominated between the 8th and 13th centuries. However, after that time, invaders from outside the region gained power.

The Ottoman Empire

By the 1500s the major influence in the Middle East was the Ottoman Empire, based in Istanbul (formerly Constantinople). The Empire was an Islamic-based government headed by a Muslim ruler—the Ottoman sultan. At the time, the Islamic religion, founded during the seventh century by the Prophet Muhammad, was the main faith throughout the region. In addition to being the highest political authority, the Ottoman sultan was also the caliph (the Arabic term for "successor," meaning the successor of the Prophet Muhammad). This meant he also wielded the highest religious authority.

During the 16th and 17th centuries, the Ottoman Empire was at the height of its power. At that time it encompassed lands in southeastern Europe

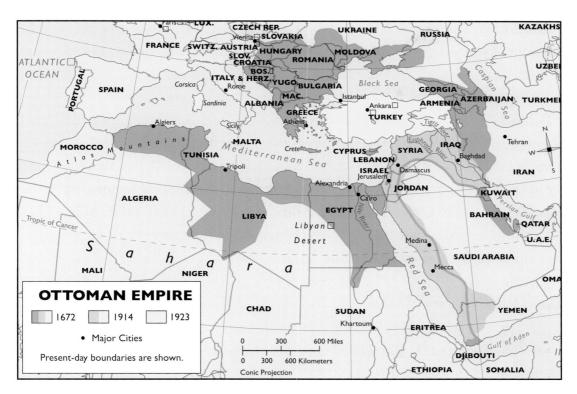

OTTOMAN EMPIRE

1672 1914 1923

• Major Cities

Present-day boundaries are shown.

0   300   600 Miles
0   300   600 Kilometers
Conic Projection

This map shows the territory ruled by the Ottoman Empire at various times in history. By the early 20th century the once-mighty Ottoman Empire had been whittled down to territory on the Anatolian Peninsula, Arabian Peninsula, and the Eastern Mediterranean.

(including all of the Balkans), Anatolia, Iraq, western Iran, Greater Syria, Egypt, the western Arabian Peninsula, and the coast of North Africa spanning from Egypt to eastern Morocco.

However, by the beginning of the 19th century, when the First World War broke out, the Ottoman Empire was on its last legs. Its former lands of Egypt and Cyprus were under British occupation. Tunis had been lost to the French. The Kars, Ardahan, and Batum provinces (of today's eastern Turkey) were under Russian control. And Greece, Romania, Bulgaria, Serbia, Montenegro, Bosnia, and Crete were all independent or autonomous.

The Ottoman Empire's decision in 1914 to align with Germany and Austria-Hungary at the beginning of the First World War would prove its final undoing. As an ally of Germany, the Empire opposed the Entente powers of Great Britain, France, and Russia, and later the United States. When the war ended in 1918, the Ottoman Empire was on the losing side. At the 1919 peace conference, the Entente powers used their victory to pick apart the remnants of the Ottoman Empire.

European Control

After the end of World War I, the European victors carved out new nations in the Middle East and established new governments, called mandates. A form of government established under and administered by the newly formed League of Nations, the mandates were supposed to allow European countries to assist in the development of new governments in areas designated for eventual independence. However many European countries used their control for their own financial benefits.

Even before the establishment of mandates, foreign nations had gained power over other parts of the Middle East. By the 1880s, the French government had claimed much of North Africa. Great Britain held power over the Persian Gulf coast, as well as Egypt and the Sudan. Both Britain and Russia were major influences in Persia (Iran).

David Lloyd George of Britain, Vittorio Orlando of Italy, Georges Clemenceau of France, and Woodrow Wilson of the United States confer outside a hotel during the Paris Peace Conference, 1919. Before the conference Wilson had proposed that nationalities living under the control of the defeated Ottoman and Austro-Hungarian empires should be allowed to rule themselves. However, the nationalist aspirations of Arabs, Jews, and others in the Middle East were put on hold by the victorious colonial powers, who sought control of the region's resources for themselves.

Nationalist Movements

During the 19th century and early 20th century, several nationalist movements evolved in the Middle East in response to Ottoman rule. Nationalist movements also developed in response to European political actions. To many Arabs, the mandate status established in the 1920s was a form of European imperialism—a system in which Arab lands were being used by foreigners and governed as colonies. A growing desire for self-rule led to the formation of numerous Arab nationalist groups calling for political sovereignty.

Arab nationalists believed that loyalty to Arabs and an Arab identity took precedence over all other loyalties, including to religion, an individual nation, or tribe. The idea of Arab nationalism would become the animating force behind significant political movements in the Middle East from the 1930s on.

Another major nationalist movement at odds with Arab nationalism was the Zionist movement (the movement to reunite the Jewish people in Palestine). The idea of the "return to Zion," whereby the dispersed Jews would gather again in their former homeland in Israel has been a central idea in Jewish thought and belief since the Jews were driven out of that area by the Roman Empire during the second century A.D. However, it was only in modern times that this idea became the practicable goal of a political movement.

Zionism—the idea of the creation of a Jewish state in what was then part of the Ottoman Empire—developed to a great extent around the same time as Arab nationalism. The goals of the Zionist and Arab nationalist movements would make the Middle East fractious and politically unstable for many decades.

Another important nationalist movement that helped shape the Middle East of today was a group that in the West (the countries of Europe and North America) was referred to as the "Young Turks." The Young Turks were a political organization, based in Istanbul, Turkey, that was first established in 1889 in direct response to governance by the Ottomans. During the early part of the 20th century, its members worked to replace the religious-based Ottoman government with a secular Turkish state modeled after the governments of the West.

Around the same time, in the country of Iran, the nationalist movement focused on the Iranian identity. It is distinct in many ways—including language, culture, and religion—from that of other countries in the Middle East.

The following pages give a historical overview of the emergence, growth, and transformation of nationalism in the Middle Eastern context. Nationalism remains a potent force in the Middle East. The passion and commitment it inspires will continue to affect the lives of the peoples of the region.

(Opposite) A meeting of the Arab League in Cairo. The league was formed in 1945 to enable several newly independent Arab states to work together. (Right) Bedouin raiders like these helped the British defeat Ottoman forces in the Middle East, believing they would gain independence in return.

2 *Early Arab Nationalism*

A rab nationalism is one of the most important political ideologies to have emerged from the historical experience of the 20th-century Middle East. The ideology is related to that of the movement known as Pan-Arabism, although Pan-Arabism differs in that it specifically calls for the formation of a single united Arab state. This Arab state would be created from the countries of the *Arab world*—the term used to describe all countries in which Arabic is the native language.

The Arab Awakening

The idea of Arab political sovereignty first emerged in the late 19th century, in the writings of Arab intellectuals seeking to achieve reforms within the Ottoman Empire. Christian Arab writers in Damascus (in present-day Syria) and Beirut (in today's Lebanon) were the first to openly demand political independence for Arabs. In 1900 Abd al-Rahman al-Kawakibi published *Characteristics of Tyranny*, an early work expressing the concept of the Arabs as a nation. In *The Awakening of the Arab Nation*, published in 1905, Syrian writer Naguib Azouri demanded the establishment of an Arab state stretching from the Arabian Sea to the Mediterranean.

The years after 1905 saw the emergence of various secret Arab nationalist societies in Damascus and Beirut promoting views similar to those expressed by Azouri. The establishment of these groups marked the real beginnings of Arab nationalist political activity. The most famous of these secret societies was the Jamiyyat al-Umma al-Arabiyya al-Fatat (the Society of the Young Arab Nation). The organization, known simply as al-Fatat, was founded in 1911 by two students studying in Paris—Awni Abd el Hadi and Mohammed Rustum. Two years later, the group organized a congress in Paris calling for reforms by Ottoman authorities. Afterward, al-Fatat moved its center of operations from Europe to Beirut and established a presence in Damascus.

1916 Arab Revolt

During World War I, al-Fatat, along with another secret Arab society, al-Ahd, worked with Hussein Ibn Ali, who was the emir of Mecca and sharif of the

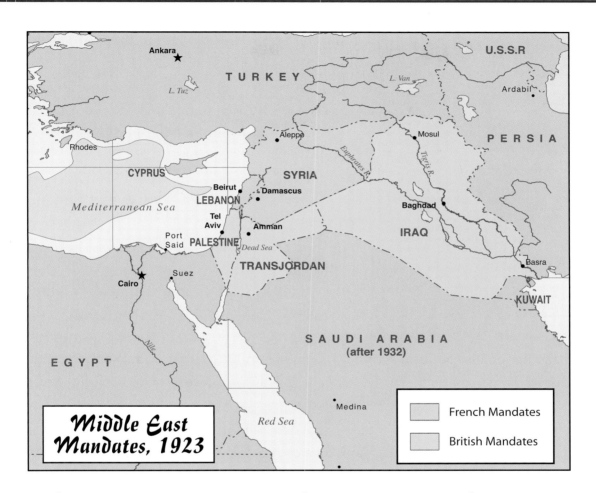

Middle East Mandates, 1923

French Mandates
British Mandates

Hashemite family, to rise up against the Ottomans. During this 1916 Arab Revolt, Hussein's cavalry and British troops drove the Ottomans from Palestine and Syria.

With the collapse of the Muslim Ottoman Empire at the end of World War I, in 1918, the question of Arab independence and statehood emerged as a

In 1920 the Syrian National Congress elected Faisal I king of Greater Syria—a proposed state that would have included the modern countries of Syria, Lebanon, Cyprus, and Israel, as well as parts of Iraq, Jordan, and Turkey. However, the League of Nations did not accept the establishment of Greater Syria, and France and Britain enforced the borders of the mandate states.

serious political issue. Faisal, the 36-year-old son of Sharif Hussein, proclaimed the establishment of a Syrian Arab kingdom—Greater Syria—with Arab nationalism as its official ideology. However, in 1920 the French occupied Damascus and forced Faisal to flee.

The British had promised the Arabs that if successful, Ottoman land would become an independent Arab state. However, despite assurances given to Hussein and his allies by the British and French, the Arab Revolt failed to produce a lasting, fully independent Arab sovereignty. Instead, the Middle East was divided among European powers to be governed as international protectorates or mandates. Britain controlled Iraq, Palestine, and present-day Jordan, while France took over Syria and Lebanon.

Subsequently, Arab nationalism became a growing force, especially in French-controlled Syria and Lebanon. During the 1920s, in the cities of Damascus and Beirut, educated young people protested against repression by the French, complaining that Arabs had been given no voice in government or civil rights. Arab nationalists also objected to the lack of progress in creating the constitutional framework for future independence as promised by the League of Nations.

Sati' al-Husri: Formulator of Arab Nationalism

In Iraq, uprisings against British rule in 1920 forced authorities to eventually allow the formation of a constitutional monarchy, with Faisal as king. However, Great Britain retained control over much of the country's internal and external political affairs.

King Faisal served as the first significant political mentor of Arab nationalism. During his reign in Iraq (1921–1933), he helped promote the ideology of Arab nationalism through the efforts of his director-general of education, Sati' al-Husri. Many scholars credit al-Husri as the key formulator of the Arab nationalist idea. He turned the vague notion of Arab ethnic pride and assertion into more than a fairly simple demand for independence—to one coupled with a basic pride in Arab language and traditions.

Al-Husri was a former Ottoman bureaucrat who came from a Syrian Muslim family. Although he would come to stress the importance of language in national identity above any other single element, Arabic was not his first language—he learned Turkish and French first. Al-Husri considered people who spoke Arabic as their mother tongue to be Arabs, defining Arab national identity in terms of language.

Through the Iraqi education system headed by al-Husri, and with the founding and growing activity of political groups, the idea of Arab nationalism

(Above) Theodor Herzl (1860–1904) founded the modern Zionist movement and worked toward the establishment of a Jewish homeland. (Opposite) After Herzl's death Chaim Weizmann (1874–1952) and other mainstream Zionist leaders pressured the British for a Jewish state in Palestine.

spread. During the 1920s and 1930s, it continued to gain in popularity among the educated middle classes.

During this time a few countries in the Middle East were enjoying a degree of independence. In addition to Iraq, they included North Yemen (1918), Egypt (1922), and Saudi Arabia (1932). An autonomous Druze state existed in the southern part of Syria as a result of the religious minority group's Great Revolt against the French in 1925. However, Syria would continue to struggle for autonomy for many more years. And while Jordan gained partial independence in 1928, decades would pass before full independence was achieved. Even after achieving independence, the new nations of the Middle East continued to be strongly influenced by the British and French.

Palestine and the Zionist Movement

The growing Arab nationalism movement was in direct conflict with the Zionist movement, which sought to create a Jewish national homeland. Zionist immigration to Ottoman Palestine is usually considered to have begun in 1882, with the arrival of members of the Bilu group, mainly consisting of students from Kharkov in today's Ukraine. Zionist immigration from Tsarist Russia occurred in response to a series of pogroms (organized massacres of people of the Jewish ethnic group), taking place in the southwestern provinces of Russia.

The founder of modern political Zionism was Theodor Herzl, a Hungarian Jewish journalist. In 1897 he organized the first Zionist Congress, which was held in Basel, Switzerland. At the Basel Congress, Herzl defined the aim of the Zionist movement as striving "to create for the Jewish People a home in Palestine secured by public law."

When the Ottoman Empire was destroyed after the First World War, influential Zionists, notably Dr. Chaim Weizmann, saw their opportunity to press Britain for a commitment to a Jewish national home. Initial British support for the movement was secured with the issuing of the Balfour Declaration on November 2, 1917. Foreign Secretary

Arthur James Balfour declared in the statement that the British government favored the "establishment in Palestine of a national home for the Jewish People."

In the subsequent years of the British administration of the Palestine Mandate, the Jewish population increased substantially, turning Jewish nationalist aspirations into a formidable force. Most of the newly arrived Jews were fleeing persecution—from Russia and Poland in the 1920s, and from Germany and other central European countries in the 1930s. In the course of the 1930s, the Jewish population almost tripled, from 46,000 in 1931, to 135,000 in 1935.

As the Jewish population increased, so a flourishing Zionist political life developed, with parties and movements representing different Zionist streams. A coalition of Labor Zionists and their allies controlled the institutions of the movement from 1931. The policy of the Labor Zionists and their allies, led by David Ben-Gurion, differed from that of their right-wing Zionist opponents. They stressed the slow, incremental buildup of the Jewish presence in the country, which would precede the open demand for statehood. Their opponents, the Revisionist Zionists of Vladimir Jabotinsky, favored the immediate announcement of statehood as the goal of Zionism, and an uncompromising political struggle towards this end. In terms of their ultimate goal of Jewish sovereignty, however, the two sides did not differ in major ways.

The 1931 Jerusalem Congress

During the early 1920s the Arabs of Palestine organized to oppose the Palestine Mandate and the Zionists. Arabs from outside Palestine also opposed the growing Jewish population in the region and wanted British authorities to restrict Jewish immigration. Another concern was that contributions from Zionists in the United States were allowing Zionists to buy Arab lands and force Arab Palestinians to leave.

In 1931 the General Islamic Congress, meeting in Jerusalem, brought together Arab nationalist activists from most Arab countries. The conference

To protest Jewish immigration into Palestine, the Arab residents of the region frequently resorted to violence. This is an anti-Zionist demonstration at Jerusalem's Damascus gate, March 1920.

was called to discuss the situation in Palestine. However, at the same time conference members issued a pan-Arab covenant by laying down general guidelines for nationalist Arab political activity.

These guidelines included a statement affirming that "the Arab countries form an integral and indivisible whole." The covenant also demanded that "all efforts in every Arab country are to be directed towards the achievement of total independence within one single unity." The statement committed the congress to oppose European colonialism, which it described as "incompatible with the dignity and paramount aims of the Arab nation," and which it vowed to resist "with all the means at its disposal."

The delegates hoped that this conference would mark the beginnings of the creation of a general congress of all Arab nations. And it was their hope that King Faisal of Iraq would support their program. This did not take place as Faisal died shortly after the conference. British opposition would have made the likelihood of his support questionable in any case.

Arab Nationalist Political Parties

Shortly after the Jerusalem Congress, former members of the al-Fatat society formed the Arab Independence Party (AIP). This party was especially concerned with the Palestinian political situation and with opposing the British mandate and the Zionist movement in Palestine. But its program was Arab nationalist—declaring the "indivisible unity" of the Arab lands to be among its principles and seeing Palestine as "an integral part of Syria."

In August 1933, the League of Nationalist Action was founded in Lebanon. Like the AIP, the League also demanded the achievement of complete indepen-

The front page of an Arab newspaper objects to a 1925 visit by Lord Arthur Balfour, the British diplomat who supported the establishment of a Jewish national home in Palestine. "Have you come to see the misfortune and misery that have befallen my country through you?" the English-language essay on the front page asks.

dence and sovereignty of the Arabs and of Arab unity. The League of Nationalist Action was significant in that it was the first to attempt to combine the issue of Arab nationalism with the issue of land reform and limiting land ownership. However, it did not gain much popular support and was defunct by 1940.

Other significant Arab nationalist organizations founded at this time include the Arab Liberation Society, the Arab Nationalist Party, and the Iraqi Nadi al-Muthanna. The latter group, founded in 1935 and based in Baghdad, tried to organize Arab nationalists from across the region. It was the first Arab nationalist organization to try to engage in the systematic ideological education of its members, producing a publication that outlined a comprehensive nationalist program.

These organizations and others like them, including secret societies, clubs, and parties, proliferated during the 1930s in Iraq. Because it was the most politically independent of the Arab countries at the time, Iraq had become the political center of Arab nationalism. However, the presence of

Grand Mufti of Jerusalem Amin al-Husseini (center, wearing white cap) and other Arab leaders are pictured before a meeting with British authorities to protest against colonial policies in Palestine, 1929.

nationalist organizations in other parts of the Arabic-speaking world was negligible. In Saudi Arabia and the Persian Gulf, an ideology that proclaimed the primacy of Arab national identity over all other loyalties, including religion, had little appeal. In North Africa too, the myriad organizations of Arab nationalism did not succeed in attracting any but a tiny number of intellectuals to their ranks.

Competing Movements

Arab nationalism was at this time only one of a number of ideologies and political orientations competing for supremacy. One of the national movement's main competitors was Islamism—the movement calling for the structuring of government and society according to the holy laws of Islam, or Sharia.

Arab nationalism was also competing against various political movements with local goals. For example, Syrian nationalist Antun Saadeh believed the people should be united by their geographical region, not by their language or religion. In 1932 he founded the Syrian Social Nationalist Party, which promoted the idea of a Syrian homeland.

The 1936 Arab Revolt in Palestine

During the 1930s the future status of the Palestine Mandate remained a key mobilizing cause for Arab nationalism. Meanwhile, the struggle between the Jewish national movement of Zionism and its Arab opponents continued to escalate.

In 1936, frustrated over the lack of action in advancing their self-rule, Palestinian Arabs began a violent uprising, which included attacks on Jews and British authorities. The goal of this uprising, known as the Great Arab Revolt, was to end Jewish immigration, ban land sales to Jews, and establish an Arab government in Palestine. The British military, Zionist forces, and Jewish civilian militias used harsh measures to crush the rebellion, which ended as World War II broke out, in 1939.

Revolt in Iraq

After the Arab Revolt had been suppressed by Britain, one of its leaders—Haj Amin al-Husseini, Grand Mufti of Jerusalem and leader of the Arab Higher Committee—made his way to Lebanon. While there, Husseini organized the largest and most significant gathering of Arab nationalists since the Jerusalem Congress of 1931. The gathering organized in Bludan, in Syria, brought together 524 delegates from across the Arab world. The sole topic of discussion was the question of Palestine.

Haj Amin next made his way to Iraq, where he arrived in October 1939. Contrary to the conditions of his entry into the country, Haj Amin became involved in Arab nationalist politics. He was instrumental in creating the alliance behind Rashid Ali al-Ghailani, who in 1941 attempted an uprising against the Iraqi monarchy in Baghdad. The Arab Nationalist Party (ANP) played a minor role in the uprising, which was led militarily by a group of officers whom Haj Amin had helped bringing to the side of Rashid Ali.

Following the uprising, ANP leader Younes al Sabawi served as Minister of Economy in the short-lived government established after the war. But the uprising was soon crushed by the British, who placed Abdulillah back in charge as regent. The British then resumed direct control of Iraq.

Little of lasting political consequence ultimately emerged from this first generation of Arab nationalist agitation. Many of the small societies and clubs, despite their ringing pan-Arab rhetoric, became involved and diminished in the petty politics of their local areas.

The Arab League

Meanwhile, the cause of Arab unity, or at least cooperation, was taking steps forward elsewhere. During the 1930s, Cairo began to emerge as an alternative to Baghdad as a hub of nationalist activity. Egypt, which was the most populous and advanced of the states of the Arabic-speaking world, became a meeting place for leaders of a number of North African countries seeking independence. The notion of Egypt as the naturally preeminent country of the Arab world began to take hold.

By 1945, as the Arab world was beginning to emerge into a new era of independence and sovereignty, Egypt was assuming the position of its natural leader. And ideas of Arab unity and cooperation were on the rise there. The first organizational framework reflecting the desire of the emergent independent Arab states for greater cooperation was the League of Arab States, founded on March 22, 1945. The seven founding members were Egypt, Saudi Arabia, Iraq, Syria, Lebanon, Yemen, and Transjordan.

The League was not a pan-Arabist body. Rather, it encouraged increased cooperation among its member states, while respecting the independence and territorial integrity of each of them. Nevertheless, many people viewed its existence as the first indication of a trend toward an Arab unity that would dominate the politics of the region in the coming years.

(Opposite) President Gamal Nasser of Egypt was the leading advocate of Arab nationalism during the 1950s and 1960s. (Right) Jordanian troops drill on the Israeli border just days before the start of the Six Day War, June 1967. The Arab defeat discredited Nasser and the pan-Arab movement he championed.

3 *Arab Nationalism After the Second World War*

*E*vents of World War II, which ended in 1945, changed the world's attitude toward Jewish immigration to Palestine. During the course of the war, Nazi Germany attempted to exterminate European Jews, and at least 6 million died. After the war ended, much of the rest of the world supported the desire of the majority of these Jewish survivors to immigrate to Palestine. However, the British had established immigration quotas for the region.

The Creation of Israel

After the war, Jewish and Arab violence against British rule in Palestine rose dramatically. No longer interested in governing the Palestine Mandate, Britain turned to the newly formed United Nations (which had replaced the League of Nations) to find a solution. On November 29, 1947, by a vote of 33 to 13, with 10 abstentions, the U.N. General Assembly voted to partition the Palestine Mandate, creating a Jewish state and a Palestinian Arab state.

The Palestinian Arab leadership rejected the plan, and intercommunal violence broke out even before the British officially pulled out on May 14, 1948. Following the official declaration of the creation of the Jewish state of Israel, armies of the Arab League countries of Egypt, Syria, Transjordan, Lebanon, and Iraq moved to destroy the new nation. Fighting ended in January 1949, with Israel proving victorious in its war of independence.

The defeat at the hands of the Israelis in the war of 1948 had a galvanizing effect on the appeal of nationalist sentiment in the Arab world. Yet, it was not the only focal point for wounded Arab pride. Another major issue was the existence of British bases and personnel on the soil of ostensibly independent Arab states such as Egypt and Iraq. Both issues would help create an atmosphere ripe for the growth of Arab nationalism.

A New Generation

A new generation of Arab nationalists emerged during the 1940s. One of the most significant was Michel Aflaq, who was born in 1910 to a middle-class Christian family in Damascus. Like al-Husri, another major Arab nationalist

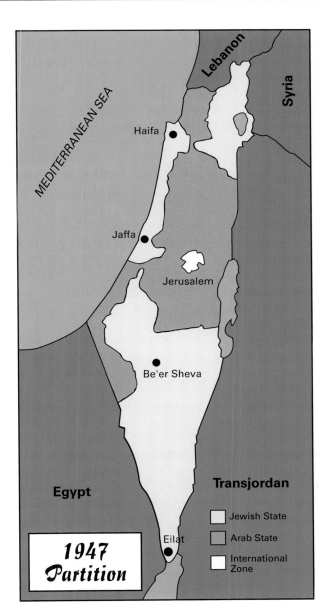

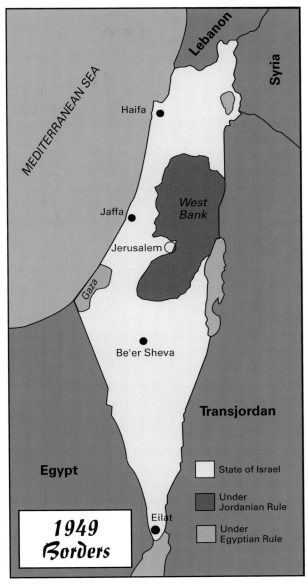

figure, Aflaq was an educationalist. He had studied in Paris before returning in 1933 to Syria, where he began a career as a teacher in government schools.

Unlike al-Husri, Aflaq was a man of the political left, and the first of his innovations would be to introduce socialism into Arab nationalist ideology.

Michel Aflaq (1910–1989) was the founder of the Baath Party, a secular political party that attempted to combine socialism with Arab nationalism. The Baath Party took power in Iraq and Syria during the early 1960s.

Socialism refers to a socioeconomic system in which property and the distribution of wealth is controlled by the state. Aflaq made clear that his form of socialism was "Arab socialism"—an ideology in which resources are shared for the good of society, but the government would not interfere with social ties that were part of Arab identity, such as traditional private ownership or inheritance.

Aflaq distinguished Arab socialism from the socialism espoused by German philosopher Karl Marx, which was the basis for communism. Marx called for class war to bring about a socialist society in which all property is publicly owned and controlled by the state. Aflaq's call was not to a particular social class. Rather, he envisaged a general Arab renaissance or rebirth (*baath*, in Arabic), which would affect not only political life, but all areas of national endeavor—economic, cultural, and moral, as well. Revolution was seen as a moral task, involving the building of the correct type of Arab individuals. Aflaq wanted to rebuild the Arab "soul," as he expressed it. He stressed faith and will as key concepts, as well as the central role of dedicated youth in the furtherance of national goals.

An additional element that marked Aflaq's nationalism from that of his predecessors was his respect for Islam. He tried to integrate it into the rather mystical sense of "Arabism" that formed the basis of his thought. Aflaq presented Islam as the greatest of the cultural creations of the Arabs—and as such, as part of a cultural heritage that could be cherished by Muslims and Christians alike.

The Baath Party

Aflaq's career in nationalist activism began in the early 1940s, when he and his close colleague, Salah al din al-Bitar, a Syrian Sunni Muslim, organized a small circle of nationalist students around themselves. Beginning in 1941, the group began to agitate against French rule of Syria, issuing leaflets in the name of *al-ihyaa al-arabi* (Arab resurrection). Beginning in late 1942, both Aflaq and Bitar devoted themselves full-time to nationalist agitation. They made some headway, and in 1946, their movement took a significant step forward when a rival nationalist leader, Zaki al-Arsuzi, and his followers elected to join forces with them.

Aflaq and al-Bitar officially founded the Baath Party in Damascus in 1947, and Aflaq was elected as its leader. It was established not as a Syrian political party but as an all-Arab one. At its first convention that year, the party expressed a doctrine that combined Pan-Arabism with a social program of agrarian reform. The idea of partial nationalization, or ownership by the state, was also supported.

The slogan of the new party was "The Arab world is an indivisible political and economic unity," or more succinctly and famously—"Unity, freedom and socialism." The party rapidly became a presence on the Syrian political scene. Branches were founded also in Lebanon, Iraq, and Jordan.

Arab Socialist Baath Party

As teachers and intellectuals, Aflaq and Bitar were inexperienced in the political campaigning necessary for the achievement of power. In 1952, their party suffered a setback when Syrian ruler Adib Shishakli banned political parties in the country.

The Baath leaders were forced into exile, where they met and joined forces with a third man whose different but complementary skills helped transform the Baath from something in the mold of an intellectual society into a real, fighting political force. Akram Haurani, leader of the Arab Socialist Party, had also been forced into exile by Shishakli. Unlike Aflaq and Bitar, Haurani was an experienced organizer with a far greater ability to speak to ordinary citizens. His party had built up a considerable following in the officer corps and among the peasantry in parts of the country.

After Shishakli was overthrown in 1954, the Baath Party and the Arab Socialist Party were merged into the Arab Socialist Baath Party. Afterward, Syria enjoyed a brief period of political pluralism in which a number of parties and movements flourished. The Arab Socialist Baath Party was one of them.

Nasser's Egypt

Meanwhile, Egypt was to play a key role in the renaissance of Arab nationalism. A major factor was the coming to power of the Free Officers, a revolutionary group led by Gamal Abdel Nasser. In 1952 the Free Officers overthrew King Farouk, whose monarchy had been supported and largely controlled by the British.

Nasser was neither an intellectual nor an ideologue by nature. He was a professional army man of humble background. First and foremost he was an Egyptian patriot. However, he also wanted to minimize the power of the former colonial powers in the region and to assert Egypt's regional leadership.

Arab nationalism became a way for the Egyptian regime to tap into and mobilize resentment of the former colonial powers and foreign interference across the region. As the Arab world's most powerful and populous state, Egypt was in many ways the natural leader of the Arabic-speaking world in the postcolonial context. Arab nationalism also provided Egypt with justification for interfering in the affairs of other states and for seeking to spread its regional influence.

During the 1950s and early 1960s, Nasser's regime enjoyed a series of foreign policy successes that further increased the Egyptian leader's charisma and the authority of the ideas he championed. One such major international incident was the Suez Crisis, which occurred in 1956 when Nasser seized the canal from the British and French companies that owned it. In response Israel, British, and French forces attacked Egypt, but later withdrew under pressure from U.S. president Dwight Eisenhower. Although Nasser's

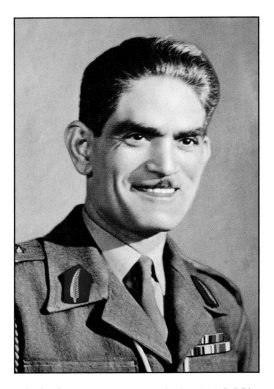

Abd al-Karim Qasim (1914–1963) emerged as the leader of Iraq after a 1958 military coup overthrew the monarchy. Qasim was a nationalist—the Hashemite rulers of Iraq had close ties to Britain and the West—but once in power he attempted to quash competing nationalist movements like the Baath Party. He was overthrown and executed in a Baath coup in 1963.

military was defeated in the course of the war, his popularity in the Arab world increased.

Another perceived achievement was Nasser's success in undermining the 1955 Western-backed alliance of Arab States, known as the Baghdad Pact (also referred to as the Central Treaty Organization, or CENTO). The agreement had been created during the Cold War by Britain, Iraq, Turkey, Iran, and Pakistan to prevent penetration into the Middle East by the Union of Soviet Socialist Republics (USSR).

Nasser opposed the Baghdad Pact. Instead, he established direct links with the Soviet Union—the enemy of the West during the Cold War.

The term *cold war* refers to a fight over ideological differences. After World War II, the Cold War conflict between the capitalist society of the United States and the communist society of the USSR had an impact on politics in countries around the world. After the Hashemite monarchy of Iraq was overthrown in 1958 in a military coup, it also developed ties with the USSR. The new regime, headed by Abd al-Karim Qasim, chose to leave the Baghdad Pact. This further diminished the pact's authority—making it perhaps the least successful Western-sponsored defense arrangement in the Cold War period.

Because of Nasser's perceived political successes during the Cold War and the message of Arab nationalism that carried throughout the region via the Cairo-based "Voice of the Arabs" radio station, many people came to identify the Egyptian leader with the idea of Arab unity. For a time in the 1950s, the prospect of Arab unity, under the guidance of Nasser's Egypt, looked like a real possibility.

The United Arab Republic

With the successes of Suez still fresh, Nasser attempted to bring about the pan-Arabic vision of a united Arab state. In 1958, Egypt was officially joined with Syria, forming the new United Arab Republic, or UAR. Nasser was the president of the new country, which had its capital in Cairo.

The union between Egypt and Syria was the culmination of the steady increase in power and influence of the Baath Party in Syria. Al-Bitar had been appointed foreign minister in 1956, and Akram Haurani had become speaker of the parliament a year later. In addition to this political strength, the Baath had won the allegiance of a network of nationalist army officers inspired by the Free Officers' regime in Egypt. In fact, the Baath Party was a prime mover in the decision for unification of the two nations.

However, troubles and friction between the Egyptian and the Syrian partners began almost immediately after unification. Among Nasser's conditions for the creation of the United Arab Republic had been the dissolution of all political parties in Syria. Aflaq, representing the Baath, had agreed to this

Cheering crowds surround an automobile carrying Egyptian president Gamal Nasser and Syrian president Shukri al-Kuwatli, who are on their way to finalize the creation of the United Arab Republic in February 1958. The union bound Egypt and Syria together to create an enormous state, appealing to many pan-Arabists. However, tensions between Egypt and Syria led to the UAR's collapse after only three years.

condition, evidently hoping to exert influence within the National Union Organization—the single political party permitted in the new United Arab Republic. The Baath was duly officially dissolved and its leaders given four ministries in the new government.

The union led to growing rifts within the Baath itself. A group of Baathist military officers, known as the Military Committee, eventually defeated the founders of the Baath Party for the leadership of the party in

Syria. One of the young officers who belonged to this group was Salah Jadid, who would go on to head the extreme left Baath regime in Syria from 1966 to 1970.

Ultimately, Nasser was not able to reach out to Syrian moderates, who had opposed the union in the first place, and he found it difficult to impose his will on the UAR partner. Proposals in December 1958 for a looser union were rejected, and the communist elements in Syria who had made them were harshly repressed. However, the proposals reflected a growing Syrian sense of chafing under foreign domination.

As a result, the UAR proved short-lived. It came to an abrupt demise on September 28, 1961, when the government in Syria was overthrown in a coup organized by moderate army officers, who were supported by the old pro-Western parties. Both al-Bitar and Haurani of the Baath supported the coup, which effectively put an end to the only serious attempt of nations to move toward Arab political unity.

The Syrian Baath Party

The failure of the UAR led to a period of radicalization in the Syrian Baath Party, which saw the ousting of the old leadership, and the rise to dominance of the Military Committee. The Baath finally ascended to power in Syria in a second military coup carried out by the party's Military Committee, in cooperation with Nasserist military officers, on March 8, 1963. Al-Bitar was made the nominal head of the government.

However, the al-Bitar government did not last out the year. By the end of 1963 the Baath, which was the only legally functioning political party in

Syria, remained torn apart by factionalism and discord. On February 23, 1966, another military coup led by Salah Jadid established a leftist, pro-Soviet Baathist regime, which managed to keep a firm grip on power in Syria. In the party purges that followed Jadid's coup, the founders of the Baath—Aflaq and al-Bitar—were themselves expelled from the party. Internal fighting in the Baath Party remained, as a nationalist faction led by Hafiz al-Assad opposed the ideas of a progressive faction supporting reform based on Marxist economics.

The tide of Arab nationalist ferment led to political instability elsewhere. In Iraq, the nationalist regime of Abd al-Karim Qasim was brought down by the Baath Party in a bloody coup in February 1963. Within the year, the Baath Party was ousted from power by a pro-Nasserite group of officers and political activists.

The Arab Cold War

Overall, after Arab nationalism's initial rush of success, rapid transformation and unification of the Arab world did not occur. Instead a dynamic developed that has been referred to by political scientist Malcolm Kerr as the *Arab Cold War*. This term refers to the period from 1958 to 1970 when a rivalry for regional influence existed between Nasser's Egypt and the conservative, Islamic regime of Saudi Arabia.

The notions of secular Arab nationalism had little appeal in Saudi Arabia and the Gulf. The Saudis had a conservative Islamist outlook and vast oil wealth—and in the larger Cold War were pro-Western. Nasser, beginning in the mid-1950s, had aligned Egypt with the Soviet side.

The Arab Cold War manifested itself in a number of regional flashpoints and crisis areas. However, the most drawn-out and costly event was the Egyptian intervention in Yemen's civil war. In 1962 Egypt sent troops into Yemen in order to give support to republican forces that opposed the monarch. Instead of the expected rapid victory, however, Egyptian forces found themselves facing pro-royalist forces that were being supported by Saudi Arabia.

Egypt became bogged down in a debilitating and brutal war that saw Egyptian forces employing chemical weapons on the battlefield. The war dragged on inconclusively. And while Nasser's Egypt still commanded the respect and loyalty of millions across the Arab world, there was a sense of waning strength of Arab nationalism as the 1960s failed to eliminate any more monarchical regimes across the region. Instead the rulers in Riyadh, Saudi Arabia, and Amman, Jordan, proved resourceful, able to mobilize international support for themselves and remain in power.

King Faisal (right) walks with Egyptian president Gamal Abdel Nasser on the way to an Arab League meeting in Cairo, 1970. Throughout the 1960s the Egyptian and Saudi regimes struggled for influence in the Arab world.

The Yemeni civil war, which lasted from 1962 to 1970, is a vivid example of how the established order proved more durable than Egypt had expected.

The Saudis offered shelter to many Egyptian Islamists fleeing Nasserite persecution. These Egyptian Islamists were able to assist the Saudis in developing their own conservative Islamist outlook as a counterweight to Nasser's pan-Arabic appeal.

The Six-Day War

The nadir of Arab nationalism came with the war against Israel in June 1967. This war was not the culmination of a carefully planned buildup, in which Arab nationalism struck at a moment of its choosing. Rather, the war was to a great extent thrust upon Nasser by events, and by action of the extremist Syrian regime of Salah Jadid. During his rule, Syria and Israel had engaged in countless border incidents in disputes over the demilitarized zone between the two countries. In April 1967, Syria shelled Israeli villages from the Golan Heights region, resulting in Israeli reprisals, and an Egyptian response that included the massing of 100,000 Egyptian troops and a thousand tanks into the Sinai Peninsula, on Israel's southern border. Nasser also organized a military alliance made up of Egypt, Syria, Jordan, and Iraq.

After a decade and more of nationalist agitation, the masses of the Arab world believed that its nationalist regimes had created armies superior to the Arab forces that had been defeated by Israel in 1948. Arab nationalism, after all, had become defined by its closeness to the military. It had portrayed the military as the key tool of development, as well as the repository of patriotic virtue. In the days leading up to the war, Cairo's Voice of the Arabs radio station delivered a steady drumbeat of propaganda promising the final defeat and destruction of the Jewish state, regarded by many Arabs as a symbol of past colonial domination.

Instead, the Arab states led by Egypt suffered a defeat of epic proportion. In six days, the army of Israel smashed the forces of Egypt, Jordan, and Syria. At the same time, Israel captured the Gaza Strip and Sinai Peninsula from Egypt, East Jerusalem and the West Bank from Jordan, and the Golan Heights from Syria.

Arab nationalism never recovered from the defeat of 1967, and the war marks, in effect, the end of its moment of dominance in the political consciousness of the region. The defeat had a number of political consequences. They included the replacement in Syria of Jadid, who was deposed by Hafiz Assad in 1970, and Egypt's turn to the West after Nasser's death the same year and his replacement by Anwar Sadat.

The Eclipse of pan-Arab Nationalism

But beyond the effects of the war on specific states, the war of 1967 marked for many Arabs the eclipse of the very idea of pan-Arab nationalism. Since al-Husri, Arab nationalism had imagined and measured success in grand, military terms. In June 1967, therefore, it had faced this test—an epic struggle on the battlefield against a historic enemy—and it had utterly failed. The success of Jewish nationalism, the subsequent suffering of the Palestinian Arabs, and the belief that Israel and Zionism represent alien, colonial implants remain important elements of the dominant political culture of the Middle East.

In a sense, Arab nationalism—and its role in motivating popular opposition and mobilizing the Arab people—has been replaced by the

Palestine Liberation Organization (PLO) chairman Yasir Arafat delivers an angry denunciation of Israel, 1972. At the same time that the mainstream pan-Arab movement was declining in the late 1960s, nationalist aspirations among Palestinian Arabs were growing stronger. Today, there remains no clear solution to the issues dividing Israel and the Palestinians.

rival ideology of Islamism. To a limited degree, the remaining partisans of Arab nationalism have found themselves in the post-1967 period seeking common ground with the more popular and powerful Islamist movements in various parts of the region.

In some ways, Islamism is similar to Arab nationalism. Both are movements that derive from a search for authenticity and from deep-seated resentment of the former colonial masters and their perceived servants. Both also place the avoidance of normalized relations with Israel close to the center of the list of their objectives.

The emergence to prominence of a separate Palestinian national movement, founded in Jerusalem in 1964 by the Arab League, has come about with the decline of a pan-Arab identity. Over the years the Palestinian cause has remained a key legitimizing symbol in Arab politics. Thus, it is both a remnant of pan-Arab solidarity and a symbol of the extent to which separate Arab identities have now emerged.

Since 1967 there has been a deepening of separate state identities. Although most of the modern Arab states are the product of colonial divides and boundary making, more than a half-century of independence has served to give increasing weight and meaning to the separate identities contained within state borders. After years of living within a nation and participating in its politics and economic activities, most citizens have developed feelings of loyalty to their particular Arab nation. They identify with their nation, and not with a pan-Arab state.

The Language of Arab Nationalism

In some Middle Eastern countries Arab nationalism survives as a sort of official political theology for a number of regimes. It has provided a language of justification for extremely oppressive regimes suffering from a lack of legitimacy.

The Baathist regime in Syria offers a good example of how this process has worked. Hafiz Assad, who came to power in 1970, succeeded in building an image for his regime as the guardian of the Arab nationalist faith. During the 30 years of his rule, he offered support and shelter for nationalist and anti-Western guerrilla and terror movements. And he chastised other Arab states for their moves toward contact and normalization of relations with Israel. By placing the country on a perceived war footing, Assad could justify his government's repressive measures used to stifle internal dissent and help preserve the regime. The language of nationalism thus served as both a reason for imposing repression, and a means for justifying it.

After the end of the First World War, Turkish nationalists battled the Allied powers to establish a new state. (Opposite) Mustafa Kemal and members of the Grand National Assembly in Sivas, 1919. (Right) Turks in traditional garb perform a folk dance. Turkish language and culture predominate in the modern state.

4 *The Nationalist Movement in Turkey*

During the late 19th century, a reformist and nationalist movement supporting the idea of a modern Turkish state in which citizens shared a common ethnic background, culture, and heritage took root within the Ottoman Empire. These nationalist Turks sought to create a secular state, as opposed to the Islamic-based Ottoman Empire.

Young Turks Take Power

In 1908, a group of Turkish officers, who would later become known in the West as "Young Turks," gained control of the government by forcing Sultan Abdul Hamid II to reestablish a parliamentary form of government. After the sultan was deposed the following year, his younger brother Mehmed V was installed as ruler, but he wielded no power. For the next 10 years, Turkish nationalists belonging to the Committee of Union and Progress controlled the government.

After the end of World War I in late 1918, Britain, France, Italy, and Greece occupied much of the Anatolian Peninsula, including the capital city of Istanbul. These countries attempted to solidify their gains in the Treaty of Sèvres, which was signed by the Entente powers and representatives of the Ottoman government on August 10, 1920.

The treaty was a total surrender on the part of the Ottoman Sultanate. The document carved up the remaining Ottoman territories into zones of occupation and several small states to be controlled by local ethnic groups—including ones for the Greeks, Armenians, and the Kurds (people native to today's southern Turkey, northern Iraq, and part of Syria).

Mustafa Kemal Pasha

However, a number of Ottoman military and parliamentary figures, led by the distinguished and charismatic commander Mustafa Kemal Pasha, gathered in the hinterlands of Anatolia. Together, they formed a national movement to liberate the Peninsula—considered the Turkish heartland—from the occupying powers.

Although they suffered large numbers of casualties, Mustafa Kemal and his colleagues proved successful on the battlefield. Within three years of the movement's first meetings, they had forced all of the European occupiers from the Anatolian peninsula. And in November 1922, their alternative government abolished the Sultanate—an event that marked the official end of the Ottoman Empire.

Now in a position of strength, Mustafa Kemal and his colleagues reentered negotiations with the Entente powers. The following year, on September 9, 1923, the Treaty of Lausanne recognized the newly formed Republic of Turkey. The terms of the treaty were much more favorable terms for Turks. However, other ethnic groups of the Ottoman Empire, including the Kurds and Armenians, did not obtain lands granted to them under the previous treaty.

Post-Independence Reforms

In contrast to many other nationalist movements, the nationalist movement in Turkey

Mustafa Kemal Atatürk (1881–1938) is considered the father of modern Turkey. His policies established Turkey as a modern, secular state with a government based on Western democratic principles.

The delegates to Lausanne, including İsmet İnönü (center), negotiated the borders of modern Turkey in 1923.

meant more than achieving political independence. Mustafa Kemal and his colleagues had more goals. Kemal introduced a wide range of measures aimed at drastically reforming the country. They followed an ideology eventually known as Kemalism or Atatürkçülük.

The first step was to come to terms with both tradition and the Islamic religion on the one hand, and modernity, industrialization, and enlightenment on the other. Kemalist leaders and intellectuals were significantly more secular and desirous of modernizing the country than the people they governed. The Kemalists sought to create a sophisticated culture with a distinctly

European flavor. To achieve this, they adopted Western legal codes, gave women the right to vote, and adopted the Western (Gregorian) calendar in place of the Islamic calendar. The traditional Arabic head covering—the fez—was outlawed, and men were encouraged to wear Western garb.

Atatürk served as president of Turkey from 1922 until his death, in 1938. During that time the newly independent country adopted European legal systems and civil codes that replaced Islamic law. This drive towards Westernization and the separation of religion from politics had significant opposition, particularly among the traditional and religious sectors of the population. In this way, Turkish nationalism differed significantly from many other nationalist movements, in which clergy and other religious leaders often played an instrumental role in the bid for independence.

Kemalists attempted to cope with this opposition by employing several strategies. For example, the term Kemalists would use to describe their new concept, *layiklik*, means something closer to *laicism* (the separation of religion from governance) rather than secularism (usually a doctrine that rejects religion and religious considerations altogether). In 1924, the Turkish Republic abolished the Ministry of Religious Affairs (along with the caliphate). The Turkish government established a Directorate of Religious Affairs, which appointed imams, preachers, sheikhs, and muezzins. The Directorate still controls virtually all religious institutions in Turkey, including mosques, mausoleums, and *tekkes* (dervish lodges).

As time passed, however, government leaders increasingly viewed the religious leaders as competitors, rather than partners, in building the new Turkey. In 1928, Mustafa Kemal took government reforms even further. That year he removed the Constitutional provision that referred to Islam as the official state religion and declared the state secular.

Thus, for Turkish nationalists trying to redefine the identity of its citizens, the religion of Islam, which itself is from the Arabic culture, was made to reflect the Turkish culture. Additional reforms included translating the Qur'an (the Islamic sacred book) and other religious books into Turkish. Certain Islamic tenets were ignored or discouraged, resulting in the increased popularity of drinking alcohol, the banning of the veil for women, and the abolishment of polygamy (marriage to more than one spouse at a time).

Forming a Turkish Identity

A primary goal of Kemalists was to foster and solidify a new national identity—one that would represent a break from the country's Ottoman past. A powerful method for reinventing the self-image of the citizenry was adopting the Western practice of using family names, or surnames. It was important that the names be Turkish ones. The most prominent example was that adopted by Mustafa Kemal, who used the name Atatürk, meaning "Father of the Turks."

Another important method for forging the new Turkish identity was to strengthen the national language. For the most part, this meant greatly reducing any Arabic, Persian, and European influences on the vocabulary. Many words were replaced with out-of-use or newly created Turkish equivalents. This process especially focused on the words used in professional fields, including technology and the sciences.

In order to facilitate the process of Turkish vocabulary development, Kemalists started holding language conferences. They also created an academic body—the Türk Dil Kurumu (Turkish Language Society)—whose dedicated purpose was to expand the vocabulary.

Turkish leaders and intellectuals decided to abandon the Arabic alphabet. Instead, the Turkish written language was to be based on the European Roman script. The Turkish desire to emulate and be considered a part of Europe influenced this move to a Latin-based alphabet. However, the new alphabet was also easier to master and better reflected the sounds of the language than its Arabic-script predecessor. (For example, the Arabic alphabet cannot represent many of the nuances in Turkish, such as the letter *ü* versus the letter *u*).

These changes to the language went hand-in-hand with a general literacy drive—a movement to increase the number of people in the country who had the ability to read and write the language they spoke. The institution of mass public education was a massive undertaking considering that literacy rates were less than 10 percent in the 1920s. The government also instituted a universal military draft (mandatory recruitment to military service), and sponsored courses in the army, thus expanding the reach of the literacy campaign.

The task of instituting mass education was especially urgent given another of the leadership's main goals: modernizing the country as quickly as possible. In addition to education reform, the leadership realized that a massive state initiative, involving intervention and regulation (what the Turks called *devletçilik*, or etatism), was necessary to create the necessary infrastructure and companies for successful economic growth. Etatism, or state socialism, involved the formation of numerous government-owned or state-supported monopolies. Given the lack of private investors with the financial capability to lead the process of economic development and modernization, state leadership was essential to bringing about quick modernization in Turkey.

Post-Atatürk Era

The period when Atatürk led Turkey was unquestionably the formative era in Turkish nationalism. Still, while much has stayed the same since he passed away in 1938, some significant changes have occurred.

The first significant changes were instituted by İsmet İnönü, Atatürk's confidant and successor as president, and had mostly to do with governing style. The years of Atatürk's rule were characterized by one-party rule by the Republican People's Party (Cumhuriyet Halk Partisi, or CHP), in which only the most senior party leaders debated foreign policy. Even then, they did so behind closed doors. Malik Mufti, a leading observer of Turkish politics, went so far as to claim that often under Atatürk "decision making was a one-man affair." As president from 1938 to 1950, İnönü opened up Turkey's political system significantly. One of his reforms was allowing for free and open multiparty elections.

Similarly, Adnan Menderes's Democrat Party (DP), which replaced İnönü's Republican People's Party in 1950, initially campaigned on a platform of liberalizing economic and political development. However, as its policies received increasing criticism, the Democrat Party government resorted to despotic measures. These included cracking down on the press; forcing out dissenters within the party; and purging civil servants, judges, and university professors suspected of being loyal to the previous political party of power, the CHP. A military intervention in 1960—launched in part

Supporters of Turkey's ruling AKP (Justice and Development) Party wave Turkish and party flags during a pre-election rally in July 2007. Despite many pressures, and occasional military interference in government affairs, Turkey remains one of the few democracies in the Middle East.

as a reaction to this authoritarianism—would lead to increased domestic political participation and civil liberties within Turkey.

The 1960 military intervention was the first of four such events. Some scholars believe it signified the continuation of the Kemalist principle that the military should serve as the guardian of the state. That is, when necessary, the military should intervene in state affairs in order to preserve the character of the state.

Despite being home to many different ethnic groups, the people of modern Iran have a strong national identity. Part of the reason for this may result from pride in Persian history and accomplishments. (Opposite) The ornate dome of a mosque. (Right) This unusual carving guards a building in Persepolis, the capital of the ancient Persian Empire.

5 *The Nationalist Movement in Iran*

Iran is a multi-ethnic mixture of peoples, with a population far more diverse than that of any Arab country. Indeed, only slightly more than half of the country's inhabitants are actually Persians, with the rest a mix of other ethnic groups, including the Azerbaijanis, Kurds, Arabs, Baluch, and Turkmen. Yet, despite its diverse ethnic background, Iran has a strong nationalist identity. Several factors have helped this strong sense of national identity to develop.

United by a Common History

One factor is the Iranian people's common history. Iran was the home of the Persian Empire, which due mainly to the conquests of Cyrus the Great during the sixth century B.C. became one of the world's most powerful empires. By the time Cyrus's grandson Darius I took the throne in 522 B.C., the empire stretched from Egypt to Afghanistan. At the height of the Persian Empire, Darius ruled more than 50 million people.

Nearly 200 years later, Macedonian king Alexander the Great defeated the forces of the massive Persian Empire and brought it to an end. After Alexander, the area had other rulers, including the Greek Seleucids, the Parthians, the Sasanians, and eventually the Islamic armies of the Saudi Arabian peninsula. By A.D. 700 these Muslim forces had established Islam as the predominant faith of the region, and Iran was under the control of the caliph of Damascus.

Unlike other Middle Eastern lands conquered by the Arab followers of Muhammad, Iran was never "Arabized," but instead retained its separate culture. While the majority of inhabitants did eventually adopt the Islamic religion of their conquerors, the masses never adopted Arabic as their spoken tongue, but instead continued to speak Persian.

United by the Shia Faith

A second factor that makes Iranians distinct from other Middle Eastern countries is that the majority (89 percent) are members of the Shia sect of Islam. Most of the rest of the Muslim world follows Sunni Islam.

While many doctrinal differences within Islam have arisen over the centuries, Shia Islam's original break from orthodox Sunni Islam centered around who was the rightful heir to Muhammad, the founder of the faith. As Muhammad had no sons to inherit his position, when he died in 632 a rift developed among Muslims based on who should succeed him—Abu Bakr, one of Muhammad's original companions, or Ali, Muhammad's son-in-law and cousin. Shi'at Ali means "partisan of Ali," and the supportors of Ali became known as the Shia. The supporters of Abu Bakr became known as the Sunni.

Ali eventually became the fourth caliph, but he was murdered, and the question of succession resurfaced. Ali's backers believed that his sons, Hassan and Husayn, were the rightful heirs; however, a rival, Mu'awiya, was eventually chosen as caliph. When Mu'awiya died, Husayn and his followers again attempted to press his claim to the caliphate, but Mu'awiya's son Yazid slaughtered them in battle in Karbala (in today's Iraq). The holiday known as Ashura commemorates these decisive events in Shia history. It is the most sacred holiday for the Shiites.

In 1501 the Shiite faith became the majority faith in Iran. At that time the region came under the control of militant religious leaders known as the Safavids. Their leader was Ismael, an extremely young, messianic leader, who conquered Iran, present-day Iraq, Azerbaijan, and the rest of the Caucuses. By 1506 he had created the vast Safavid Empire, which included all of these lands. In the midst of his conquests, the young leader declared Shia Islam to be the state religion. In doing so, he created the first Shia state. Ismael's true success, however, was not simply that Shia Islam was the official state religion, but that he succeeded in imposing it on the vast majority

Iranian Shiites perform a religious ritual outside a mosque in Tehran during the holy period known as Ashura. Iran is one of the few places where Shiite Muslims are a majority, and the shared religious beliefs have contributed to unity among the various ethnic groups living in the country.

of his populace—most of whose descendents still belong to the Shia sect of Islam today.

United by Distrust of Foreigners

Yet another factor that unites Iran's people is their distrust of foreigners and concern that foreigners are controlling the fate of their nation. While Iran's history is full of periods when their lands were overrun by foreign invaders, what forms Iranian national consciousness most in this respect is their experience since the 1800s. At that time the various tribes and ethnic groups—Persian, Azerbaijanis, Kurds, Bakhtiari, Qashqai, and many others—lived under the rule of the Qajars.

The Qajar dynasty was founded by Agha Muhammad Shah, a Turkish tribal chief who took the crown as king, or shah, in 1795. The Qajars were one of the least competent dynasties to ever rule the country. The second Qajar shah, Fath Ali Shah, fought several wars against the Russians, when the Russian Empire looked to expand southward to gain access to the Persian Gulf and the Indian Ocean. The two wars fought against Russia, from 1804 to 1813 and from 1826 to 1828, were disastrous failures and resulted in the loss of significant territory in the Caucasus Mountains and central Asia. More land was lost in 1857 after hostilities with Britain forced the Qajars to cede all claims to Afghanistan.

In addition to their incompetence in the military realm, the Qajars had no sense of fiscal responsibility, and their luxurious lifestyles, corruption, and general fiscal ineptitude led Iran into financial ruin. To stave off creditors and maintain their lavish lifestyle, the Qajars sold various economic concessions to Russia and England, granting them land rights and exclusive control over supply and trade in certain commodities. These concessions simply worsened Iran's economy and further indebted the regime.

The situation reached a climax in 1891, when Qajar ruler Nasir al-Din Shah granted a British corporation the monopoly for the production, domestic sale, and export of tobacco. The action set off a wide-scale revolt. Protests, boycotts, and demonstrations involved the full spectrum of Iranian society—

Iranian nationalists did not approve of concessions granted by Qajar ruler Nasir al-Din Shah (1831–1896), and other involvement with Western countries like Great Britain and Russia.

including merchants, peasants, clerics, and Westernized intellectuals. The revolt was successful, and the shah was forced to repeal the concession the following year. The tobacco protest and the success of the protest showed the Iranian people that popular action could bring results.

Public discontent with the Qajar government and concerns about growing foreign intervention in Iran led many people to clamor for more reforms. Among the protesters were those who had been educated in Europe, as well as some members of the government. The country needed to be modernized, European interference and influences reduced, and a constitutional government put into place, they demanded.

Evolution of Nationalism

Many writers of the 1890s expressed dissatisfaction with the Qajar government and insisted that it resist the influence of European powers. Among them were

Westernized intellectuals such as Mirza Malkum Khan (1833–1908), who published a newspaper in London, England, that criticized the Qajar government and promoted the need for constitutional reform in Iran. Other writers advocating reform during the 1890s included Fath Ali Akhundzadeh, Mirza Aqa Khan Kirmani, and Abd al-Rahim Talibov.

After Nasir al-Din Shah was assassinated in 1896, he was succeeded by Muzaffar Al-Din Shah, another Qajar ruler whose actions continued to worsen the fiscal situation in Iran. He continued the policy of incurring loans from European interests so that he could continue to live a lavish lifestyle. Some Iranians expressed their discontent by distributing protest leaflets urging governmental reform. Called *shab-namehs* (or night letters, because they were handed out at night), these protest letters demanded an end to growing European intrusion in Iran.

Foreign influence in Iran remained strong. In 1901, a British citizen named William Knox D'Arcy was granted 60-year rights to drill in a large region of Iran. The D'Arcy Oil Concession would eventually lead to the formation in London of the Anglo-Persian Oil Company, founded in 1909. Many Iranians believed that by granting those rights, the government was allowing the natural resources of Iran to be exploited.

In 1905 a six-year revolution broke out in Iran, in which merchants, artisans, and the *ulama* (the community of Muslim religious leaders) began an effort to place constitutional restrains on the Qajar government. In July 1906 protesters called for the establishment of a constituent assembly, a demand that the shah was forced to accept the following month. The new assembly met in October 1906 to write up a constitution for Iran. Ultimately, the new government placed heavy restrictions on the powers of the shah, and established a parliament, or Majlis.

The following year Muhammad Ali Shah came into power. Supported by the Russians and by conservative Shiite leaders, he closed the Majlis and suspended the constitution in 1908. In the course of his attempt to overthrow the Majlis, Muhammad Ali arrested and executed the movement's leaders.

In the meantime, Russia and Britain had signed an agreement that gave the British influence over Iran's south, while Russia was unopposed in the north—leaving the center for the Iranians themselves. The two foreign governments played crucial roles in the ongoing internal conflicts between the shah and constitutionalists. At first Russia backed the shah, but then turned on him in 1909, occupying Tabriz to save it from having to surrender to the shah's forces.

In July 1909 the constitutionalists declared a victory, deposing Muhammad Ali and replacing him with his nine-year-old son, Ahmad. A new Majlis was convened, but it was dominated by the wealthy, and not as inclusive as the first Majlis had been. Many of its members were liberal reformers who looked to create a more secular country.

Ahmad would be the last Qajar shah. His reign saw decreasing central government authority and increased rebellion within Iran. With the outbreak of World War I in 1914, Iran saw further foreign intervention in its affairs. Disapproving of an American economic advisor brought in to straighten out the country's finances, Russia and Britain occupied parts of Iran. The foreign occupation undermined the power of the Majlis, eventually forcing the parliament to adjourn in 1915. It would not meet again for another five years. The government under the shah was restored, although it was severely weakened.

Ongoing Foreign Interference

During World War I, this pattern of interference by foreigners continued as various forces fought across Iran, wreaking enormous havoc on the country. In 1921, a military commander named Reza Khan seized power in the capital city of Tehran. He eventually took over as shah, reuniting the country and embarking on a program of reforms similar to those imposed in Turkey by Atatürk. While Reza Khan succeeded in making tremendous reforms in infrastructure, health care, education, and the military, his rule was repressive. However it was foreign governments that forced Reza Shah from power—in August 1941, when Russian (now part of the USSR) and British forces invaded the country.

Following World War II, the United States forced a Soviet withdrawal from Iran. In 1953, the Central Intelligence Agency helped the British and Reza Shah topple the popular Prime Minister, Muhammad Mosaddeq. This intervention, combined with continued American support of the increasingly despotic shah throughout his reign, eventually turned Iranian public opinion against the United States.

In recent years the populist Iranian president Mahmoud Ahmadinejad has emphasized pride in national accomplishments in order to rally support for Iran's clerical government, and to justify its pursuit of nuclear weapons despite the opposition of the international community. Thus nationalism remains an important aspect of Iranian life.

Arab Nationalism and Zionism

1897: First Zionist Congress is held in Basel, Switzerland.

1900: Abd al-Rahman al-Kawakibi publishes *Characteristics of Tyranny*, an early work expressing the concept of the Arabs as a nation.

1905: Naguib Azouri publishes *The Awakening of the Arab Nation*.

1906: Students in Damascus found the Arab Renaissance Society, the first of a large number of nationalist secret societies.

1913: The Society of the Young Arab Nation organizes a congress in Paris intended to force reform on Ottoman authorities.

1914: World War I begins; the Ottoman Empire sides with Germany and Austria-Hungary against Great Britain, France, Russia, and later the United States.

1916: The Arab Revolt of Sharif Hussein Ibn Ali begins.

1917: The Balfour Declaration commits Britain to helping create a Jewish homeland in historic Palestine.

1918: World War I ends with the defeat of the Ottoman Empire. Faisal, son of Sharif Hussein, proclaims the establishment of a Syrian Arab kingdom.

1920: The League of Nations gives mandate to British to administer Iraq; France creates administrative district of Greater Lebanon within the Syrian mandate and forces Faisal to flee Damascus.

1921: Faisal becomes king of Iraq.

1922: The League of Nations officially approves the British mandate in Palestine and French mandate for Syria; Egypt gains independence.

1931: The General Islamic Conference brings together nationalist activists from all Arab countries; attendees found the Arab Independence Party.

1932: The Kingdom of Saudi Arabia gains independence; British mandate in Iraq ends and the country becomes independent.

1933: The League of Nationalist Action is founded in Lebanon.

1935: The Nadi al-Muthanna group is founded in Iraq.

1936–39: The Arab Revolt targets the Zionist movement and authorities of British rule in Mandate Palestine.

1939: A congress of Arab nationalists held in Bludan, Syria, brings together 524 delegates from across the Arab world. World War II begins.

1941: A revolt against the British in Iraq is led by Rashid Ali al-Ghailani.

1945: The League of Arab States is founded. World War II ends and the United Nations is formed.

1947: The Baath Party is founded in Damascus. The United Nations votes to partition Palestine into separate Arab and Jewish states.

1948: The United Nations establishes the State of Israel. Syria, Egypt, Jordan, and Lebanon attack Israel in the first Arab-Israeli war.

1949: Israel wins the war against the Arab countries.

1952: The organization known as Free Officers overthrows King Farouk in Egypt in a military coup. A republic is established the following year.

1954: Gamal Abdel Nasser assumes leadership in Egypt. The Baath Party merges with the Arab Socialist Party to form the Arab Socialist Baath Party.

1956: Nasser becomes president of Egypt. He nationalizes the Suez Canal, which leads to attacks by Britain, France, and Israel.

1958: The Hashemite monarchy in Iraq is overthrown by Abd al-Karim Qasim. Syria and Egypt unite to form United Arab Republic (UAR).

1961: The UAR is dissolved.

1962: Egyptian intervention in Yemen civil war begins.

1963: The Baath Party seizes power in Syria. It also comes to power in Iraq, but is deposed nine months later.

1966: The Baathist regime led by Salah al-Jadid comes to power in Syria.

1967: Syria, Egypt, and Jordan are defeated by Israel in the Six-Day War.

1970: Jadid is overthrown in Syria by Hafiz Assad, who replaces Arab nationalist policies with a more cautious, Syria-centered outlook.

1970: Nasser dies, and is replaced by Anwar Sadat, who leads Egypt toward a guarded, pro-Western policy.

Nationalism in Turkey

1908: Young Turks lead a revolt against the Ottoman government.

1918: World War I ends with an Ottoman defeat.

1922: A Greek invasion army is repulsed under the leadership of Mustafa Kemal (later named Atatürk).

1923: The Republic of Turkey is officially formed with Atatürk as president.

1938: Atatürk dies. İsmet İnönü is elected president.

1946: The Democrat Party (DP) officially registers as a political party, as Turkey moves from a one-party to multiparty system.

1950: The DP wins the majority in free elections; Celal Bayar becomes president and DP founder Adnan Menderes becomes prime minister.

1960: After the Menderes government places the country under martial law, members of the Turkish military stage a coup.

Nationalism in Iran

700: Islamic forces establish control over Iran, bringing their faith with them.

1501: The Safavid Empire conquers the region and establishes Shia Islam as the official religion.

1795: The Qajar dynasty, founded by Turkish tribal chief Agha Muhammad, comes to power.

1891: Discontent with the Qajar government results in wide-scale revolt.

1905: Revolution against the Qajar government breaks out; activists demand establishment of constitutional government.

1906: Iran's first parliament—the Majlis—is established.

1907: Russia and Britain sign an agreement to share influence in Iran.

1908: Muhammad Ali Shah closes the Majlis and suspends the constitution.

1909: Muhammad Ali is deposed and the Majlis reconvenes.

1921: Persian Cossacks Brigade officer Reza Khan seizes power in Tehran.

1925: Establishment of Pahlavi dynasty under Reza Shah Pahlavi.

73

autonomy—self-government, or the right of self-government.

Baath Party—from the Arabic word for renaissance, or rebirth; a political party founded in the 1940s in Syria and based on the ideology of Pan-Arabism.

caliph—title for the successor of Muhammad as the spiritual and political leader of Sunni Islam after Muhammad; in the Ottoman Empire, the sultan held the title of caliph.

communism—socialist ideology derived from German philosopher Karl Marx calling for class war to bring about a society in which all property is publicly owned and controlled by the state.

concession—the right to a commercial operation or to land for a specific purpose that is granted by the government.

ideologue—a person who strongly supports and promotes a set of ideas.

ideology—system of ideas and beliefs, particularly of political theory and policy.

imperialism—policy or practice of a foreign government of extending political and economic control over other lands.

Islam—the Muslim faith, which was founded by the Prophet Muhammad in the 7th century A.D.

Islamism—a reform movement advocating the restructuring of government and society in accordance with laws prescribed by Islam.

mandate—authorization given by the League of Nations for its member nations (such as France or Great Britain) to administer a territory after World War I.

mufti—Muslim jurist; an expert on Islamic religious law.

Muslim—follower of Islam.

Nasserism—an Arab nationalist political ideology based on the views of Gamal Abdel Nasser that was a major influence in the 1950s and 1960s.

nationalism—the desire by a people who share a language and culture to gain a politically independent state of their own; a collective identity based on family lineage, geographical location, religion, language, and other factors.

Pan-Arabism—an ideology based on uniting the countries of the Arab World.

pasha—Turkish officer of high rank.

protectorate—a nation that is controlled and protected by another state.

secular—describing activities and attitudes with no religious basis or connection.

Sharia—traditional laws of Islam.

Shia—one of the two main branches of Islam, or a Muslim who follows the teachings of this sect.

socialism—economic and political ideology in which the production and distribution of goods is owned or controlled by the collective group or the state.

sovereignty—authority or right of a state to govern itself or another state.

Sunni—one of two main branches of Islam, or a Muslim who follows the teachings of this sect.

Zionism—the modern national movement of the Jewish people.

Choueiri, Youssef M. *Arab Nationalism: A History*. Oxford, England: Blackwell, 2001.

Dawisha, Adeed. *Arab Nationalism in the Twentieth Century: From Triumph to Despair*. Princeton, N.J.: Princeton University Press, 2002.

Grosby, Steven. *Nationalism: A Very Short Introduction*. New York: Oxford University Press, 2005.

Halliday, Fred. *The Middle East in International Relations: Power, Politics and Ideology*. Cambridge, England: Cambridge University Press, 2005.

Hourani, Albert. *A History of the Arab Peoples*, London: Faber and Faber, 1991.

Kayali, Hasan. *Arabs and Young Turks: Ottomanism, Arabism, and Islamism in the Ottoman Empire, 1908-1918*. Berkeley: University of California Press, 1997.

Khalidi, Rashid et al., eds., *The Origins of Arab Nationalism*, New York: Columbia University Press, 1991.

Khoury, Philip S. *Urban Notables and Arab Nationalism: The Politics of Damascus 1860–1920*. Cambridge, England: Cambridge University Press, 2003.

Provence, Michael. *The Great Syrian Revolt and the Rise of Arab Nationalism.* Austin: University of Texas Press, 2005.

Watenpaugh, Keith David. *Being Modern in the Middle East: Revolution, Nationalism, Colonialism, and the Arab Middle Class*. Princeton, N.J.: Princeton University Press, 2006.

http://www.ciaworldfactbook.com

The CIA World Factbook provides basic facts and figures on countries around the world, include those of the Middle East.

http://www.mideastinfo.com

The Middle East Information Network site provides information on education, religion, news stories, business and various countries of the region.

http://www.wnmideast.com/

Provides news information from the World News network for the Mideast region, with links providing access to general information, or for specific countries or cities.

http://www.arabworldnews.com/

Provides news information from the World News network for the Arab World.

Numbers in **bold italic** refer to captions.

Contributors

Jonathan Spyer is a Senior Research Fellow at the Global Research in International Affairs Center, in Herzliya, Israel. He holds a PhD in International Relations from the London School of Economics. His articles and analysis of political processes in the modern Middle East are published widely, and he is a regular contributor to the *Guardian* and *Haaretz* newspapers.

Cameron S. Brown is the Deputy Director of the Global Research in International Affairs (GLORIA) Center. He is the author of more than a dozen academic articles on various Middle Eastern issues in such publications as *Middle East Journal, The Review of International Studies, Israel Affairs, Turkish Studies*, and *MERIA Journal*.

Picture Credits